Recycling

Paper

Kate Walker

Marshall Cavendish
Benchmark
New York

This edition first published in 2011 in the United States of America by
Marshall Cavendish Benchmark
An imprint of Marshall Cavendish Corporation

Website: www.marshallcavendish.us

This publication represents the opinions and views of the author based on Kate Walker's personal experience, knowledge, and research. The information in this book serves as a general guide only. The author and publisher have used their best efforts in preparing this book and disclaim liability rising directly and indirectly from the use and application of this book.

Other Marshall Cavendish Offices:
Marshall Cavendish International (Asia) Private Limited, 1 New Industrial Road, Singapore 536196 • Marshall Cavendish International (Thailand) Co Ltd. 253 Asoke, 12th Flr, Sukhumvit 21 Road, Klongtoey Nua, Wattana, Bangkok 10110, Thailand • Marshall Cavendish (Malaysia) Sdn Bhd, Times Subang, Lot 46, Subang Hi-Tech Industrial Park, Batu Tiga, 40000 Shah Alam, Selangor Darul Ehsan, Malaysia

Marshall Cavendish is a trademark of Times Publishing Limited

All websites were available and accurate when this book was sent to press.

Library of Congress Cataloging-in-Publication Data

Walker, Kate.
    Paper / Kate Walker.
      p. cm. — (Recycling)
    Includes index.
    Summary: "Discusses how paper is made and the variety of ways to recycle
    it"—Provided by publisher.
    ISBN 978-1-60870-132-2
    1. Waste paper—Recycling—Juvenile literature. I. Title.
    TS1120.5.W35 2011
    676'.142—dc22
                        2009041324

First published in 2009 by
MACMILLAN EDUCATION AUSTRALIAN PTY LTD
15–19 Claremont Street, South Yarra 3141

Visit our website at www.macmillan.com.au or go directly to www.macmillanlibrary.com.au

Associated companies and representatives throughout the world.

Edited by Julia Carlomagno
Text and cover design by Christine Deering
Page layout by Christine Deering
Photo research by Legend Images
Illustrations by Gaston Vanzet

Printed in the United States

Acknowledgments
The author and the publisher are grateful to the following for permission to reproduce copyright material:

Front cover photograph: Boy and girl recycling paper, photo by Stockbyte/Getty Images

Photos courtesy of: © Lourens Smak/Alamy, 13 left; Coo-ee Picture Library, 15, 18 bottom left and bottom right; David Porter School, 28, 29; © Hotduckz/Dreamstime.com, 30 center; © swq/Fotolia.com, 30 top; Dev Carr/Getty Images, 14; Photodisc/Getty Images, 12 right; RL Productions/Getty Images, 4; David Silverman/Getty Images, 12 center; Stockbyte/Getty Images, 1; © Missing35mm/iStockphoto.com, 30 bottom; © Greg Nicholas/iStockphoto.com, 18 top; © Ralph125/iStockphoto, 5; © 2008 Jupiterimages, 17; MEA Photo, 3, 22; © Peter E. Smith, Natural Sciences Image Library, 12 left; PaperlinX Office, 13 right; Photolibrary/Randy Faris, 6; Photolibrary/David R Frazier, 9 all; Photolibrary/Elfi Kluck, 21; Photolibrary/Radius Images, 16; Shutterstock, 7; © Dana Bartekoske/Shutterstock, 26; © Countryroad/Shutterstock, 23; © Les Scholz/Shutterstock, 20; © Annamaria Szilagyi/Shutterstock, 8; Copyright 2006 Yellow Woods Challenge UK, 27.

While every care has been taken to trace and acknowledge copyright, the publisher tenders their apologies for any accidental infringement where copyright has proved untraceable. Where the attempt has been unsuccessful, the publisher welcomes information that would redress the situation.

1 3 5 6 4 2

Contents

Glossary Words

When a word is printed in **bold**, you can look up its meaning in the Glossary on page 31.

What Is Recycling?

Recycling is collecting used products and making them into new products. Recycling is easy and keeps the environment clean.

Every piece of paper that is recycled saves resources and helps the environment.

Why Recycle Paper?

Recycling paper helps:

- save **natural resources** for future use
- reduce **pollution** in the environment
- keep waste material out of **landfills**

If more paper was recycled, landfills such as this one could be closed.

Paper Products

People use many different paper products every day. Paper is used in:

- paper towels
- tissues
- paper bags
- toilet paper
- cardboard boxes

Paper towels can be used to wipe up messes.

Even though many people use computers, most people still use a lot of paper. Paper is used in:

- notebooks
- books
- newspapers
- magazines

Many people use paper to print documents.

How Paper Is Made

Paper is made from wood, which comes from trees. Trees are a natural resource that can be replaced. However, trees are now being cut down faster than new ones can grow.

Trees are cut down to be made into paper.

The Paper-Making Process

Wood goes through a three-stage **process** called **pulping** to make paper.

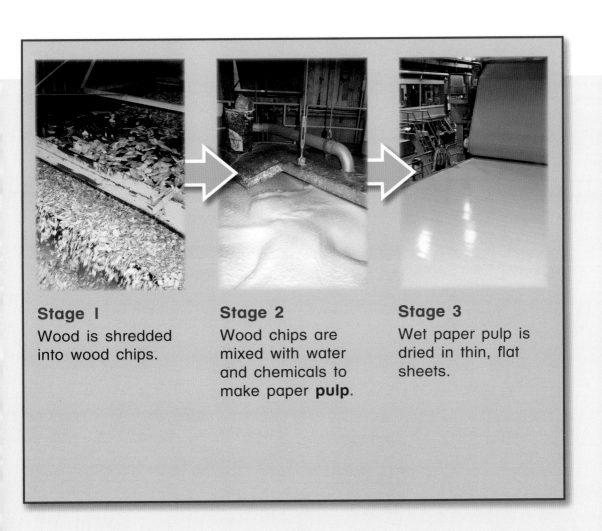

Stage 1
Wood is shredded into wood chips.

Stage 2
Wood chips are mixed with water and chemicals to make paper **pulp**.

Stage 3
Wet paper pulp is dried in thin, flat sheets.

Throwing Away Paper or Recycling Paper?

Throwing away paper uses natural resources, increases pollution, and adds to waste.

Which Resources Are Lost When Paper Is Thrown Away?	
Natural Resources	• More trees are cut down • More power is used to shred wood • More water is used to make paper pulp
Pollution	• Harmful chemicals are released into rivers and the air
Waste	• More land is used for landfills

Recycling paper saves natural resources, reduces pollution, and cuts down waste. Which do you think is better, throwing away or recycling paper?

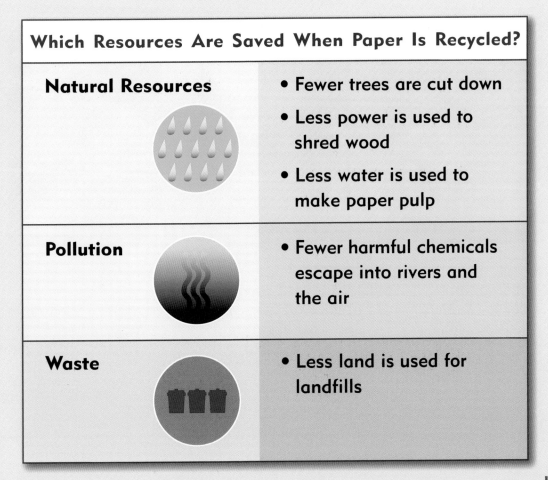

Which Resources Are Saved When Paper Is Recycled?

Natural Resources	• Fewer trees are cut down • Less power is used to shred wood • Less water is used to make paper pulp
Pollution	• Fewer harmful chemicals escape into rivers and the air
Waste	• Less land is used for landfills

How Paper Is Recycled

Paper is recycled through a five-stage process. This process begins when we recycle used paper. It ends with new paper products.

Stage 1
Used paper is collected from recycling bins left at the curb.

Stage 2
Different types of paper are separated into **pure streams**.

Stage 3
Paper is shredded and mixed with water to make paper pulp. Chemicals are added to the paper pulp to remove ink and glue.

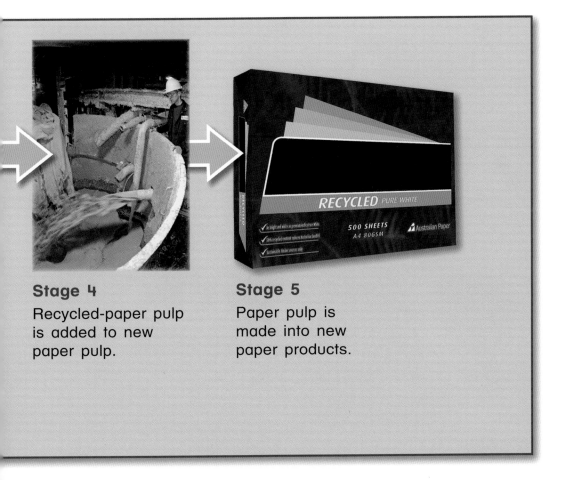

Stage 4
Recycled-paper pulp is added to new paper pulp.

Stage 5
Paper pulp is made into new paper products.

Recycling Paper at Home

Most households in towns and cities have special recycling bins. All **recyclable** paper and cardboard can be put into these bins.

Paper is put into recycling bins, which will be emptied by recycling trucks.

How to Recycle Paper

The correct way to recycle paper is:

- keep paper dry
- remove any metal clips, except staples
- keep plastic bags out of recycling bins

Remove metal clips from paper before recycling it.

Recycling Paper at School

Schools use paper for lesson sheets, taking notes, and craft activities. Most classrooms have a paper-recycling bin. A team of **monitors** looks after the bin.

A classroom recycling bin reminds students to recycle all used paper.

Paper-Recycling Monitors

Paper-recycling monitors:

- take turns emptying the recycling bin
- remind classmates to keep recycling paper
- check that only recyclable paper has gone into the recycling bin

These paper-recycling monitors are responsible for checking that newspapers are recycled.

Can All Paper Be Recycled?

Not all paper can be recycled. Paper coated with wax or plastic is **nonrecyclable**. Removing wax and plastic from paper costs too much.

Fluorescent paper, food-stained paper, and paper coated in wax or plastic should go in the garbage can.

Paper **contaminated** with food or oil is also nonrecyclable. Food and oil cause problems in the paper-pulping process.

Which Types of Paper Are Recyclable?

Recyclable paper	Nonrecyclable paper
✔ white printer paper	✘ plastic-coated paper
✔ newspapers	✘ wax-coated cardboard
✔ envelopes	✘ fluorescent paper
✔ egg cartons	✘ food-soiled paper or cardboard, such as pizza boxes
✔ cardboard	✘ tissues

Is Recycling Paper the Best Option?

Recycling paper saves trees and helps the environment. However, recycling paper also uses resources. A lot of water is used to turn recycled paper into paper pulp.

Recycling paper uses water, which is a valuable natural resource.

Trucks that collect paper for recycling burn
fossil fuels in their engines. Burning fossil fuels
causes air pollution.

Paper-recycling trucks burn fossil fuels, which causes air pollution.

Reducing and Reusing Paper

There are many ways to reduce paper use and to reuse paper. One way is to write on both sides of every sheet.

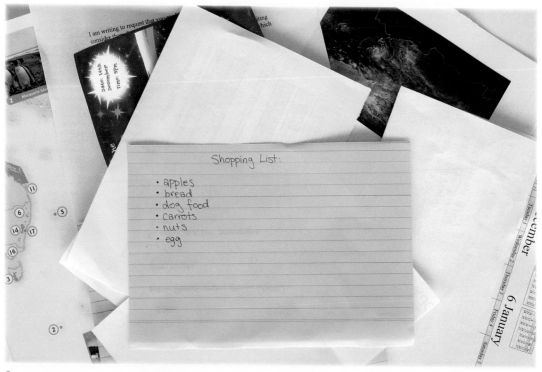

An easy way to reduce paper use is to use every sheet of paper twice.

Some simple ways to reuse paper are:
- cut scrap paper in half and staple the pieces together to make notepads
- recycle old cards to create new handmade cards
- use envelopes more than once

Pictures from old holiday cards can be used to create new cards.

Make a Box Town

Some foods come in cardboard boxes. Build a town using food boxes of different shapes and sizes.

What You Will Need:
- different-sized food boxes
- cardboard tubes of different lengths
- paints
- a marker
- scissors
- glue

What to Do:

1. Paint the boxes different colors.

2. Draw doors and windows on the boxes with a marker.

3. Glue cardboard tubes to some boxes to make chimneys. Tape it to the box until the glue dries.

4. Arrange the boxes to form a town. Cut out treetop shapes and glue them to cardboard tubes to make trees.

School Recycling Projects

In the United Kingdom, many schools collect old telephone directories for recycling. The paper is recycled into animal bedding, egg cartons, cardboard, and newspapers.

Old directories are replaced each year with new books containing updated telephone numbers.

Schools that collect the greatest number of telephone directories win cash prizes. Some students use the telephone directories to make giant sculptures before the books are recycled.

Milton Junior School students made this owl sculpture from old telephone directories.

Cozy Comfort Pillows

Students at the David Porter School in Little Neck, New York, are prize-winning **recyclers**. They won a Super Recyclers Award for their Cozy Comfort Pillows.

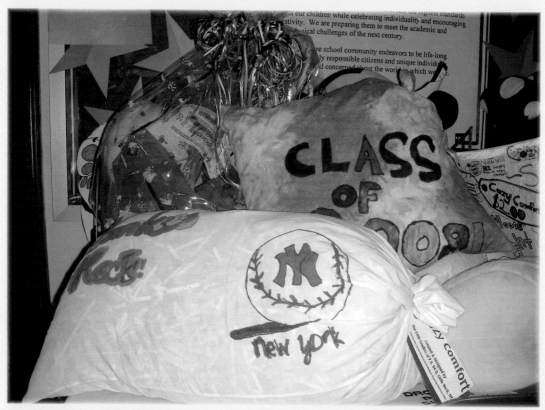

Students at the David Porter School made Cozy Comfort Pillows with used paper.

Students used shredded classroom paper to stuff their hand-decorated pillows. They also made doorway draft stoppers with used paper.

David Porter School students made draft stoppers, called Cozy Comfort Critters, with used paper.

How Recycling Paper Helps Animals

Paper is made from trees. Cutting down trees destroys animal **habitats**. When you recycle paper you save the habitats of many animals, including:

- koalas

- tree snakes

- owls

Glossary

contaminated Ruined by small amounts of harmful material.

fossil fuels Oil-based fuels that power engines in cars and trucks.

habitats Areas where animals live, feed, and breed.

landfills Large holes in the ground where garbage is buried.

monitors Students who are given special duties.

natural resources Materials found in nature that people use and value.

nonrecyclable Not able to be recycled.

pollution Waste that damages the air, water, or land.

process A series of actions that brings about a change.

pulp A thick paste-like mixture, similar to papier-mâché.

pulping A process that turns wood chips, water, and chemicals into paper pulp.

pure streams Groups of items made of the same material.

recyclable Able to be recycled.

recyclers People who recycle.

Index